SHOULDER TAP

MAURICE RIORDAN

Shoulder Tap

faber

First published in 2021
by Faber & Faber Ltd
Bloomsbury House
74–77 Great Russell Street
London WC1B 3DA

First published in the USA in 2021

Typeset by Hamish Ironside
Printed in the UK by TJ Books Ltd, Padstow, Cornwall

A CIP record for this book is available from the British Library

ISBN 978-0-571-36711-5

2 4 6 8 10 9 7 5 3 1

How can a man be born when he is old?
                                    – John 3:4

for Frank

Acknowledgements

Thanks are due to the editors of the following publications, where some of these poems appeared: *Agenda, Bad Lilies, Dark Horse, Irish Times, Magma, New Statesman, Ploughshares, PN Review, Poetry, Poetry Ireland Review, The Poetry Review, Southword, Spectator*.

I am grateful to Christopher Reid for permission to 'steal' the Turnip/Trump pun (twice) from his *Not Funny Anymore* (Rack Press, 2019). Sincere thanks to Matthew Hollis, my editor at Faber, for his dedicated support; and to his colleagues Lavinia Singer, Rali Chorbadzhiyska and Hamish Ironside. Thanks to Patrick Crotty and Emily Berry for editorial suggestions. My warmest thanks to Kathryn Maris for her critical ear and constant encouragement while writing the book.

Contents

I'm working at night by the light of my iPhone
like I'm copying that feat of Fillan the Culdee's
copying the Gospel by the light of his arm-bone.
I'm working at night by the light of my iPhone.
Fillan (I'm guessing) kept a phosphorescent stone
up his sleeve, the saint whose airborne bell was flown
by an Angel – or crow he had tamed for the wheeze?
I'm working at night by the light of my iPhone.
Like I'm copying that feat of Fillan the Culdee's.

The Changeling

After they found me hiding in a fork of the yew
I climbed into the chimney of the derelict house.
Curled in the bend, I saw the blue hole of the sky.
I liked silos, undersides of bridges, fields of dense maize.
I clambered onto bales to smoke against the barn roof.
Later, I lay down in a high-sided trailer and went to sleep.
When I woke I was out on the bare dunes under stars.

At school I lurked in the ball alley after lights-out,
or in the chapel by the glow from the tabernacle.
I thought you can hide in galleries and foreign cities,
in bars in daytime, even in a swimming pool.
There are hours you can spend loosely tethered to a lover.
There's the solace of watching over a sleeping baby.
The peace at night in the company of a dead body.

During the Recent Thunder & Lightning

I

There was the prandial-comfort of entertaining a few old
cronies.
The assurance, when the power went, each friend round
the table
was entertaining thoughts as infantile and forbidden as
my own.
One friend is convinced we're players in a computer game.
She and I argued the toss. Now happily I entertain the thought
I came into existence on or about Easter Sunday 1983.
Fully formed and complete with a plausible 30-year backstory.
It includes the smell of carbide, a rare blood type, a broken
heart.

II

There was the amnion-comfort of lying in bed as the storm
peaked.
The wish to watch a physical disaster unfolding in real time.
To witness the spectacle of ball-lightning entering an office
tower
or a plane exploding from the yellow cloud above the sports
ground.
The incipient desire, then, for catastrophes on a truly grand
scale.
The sort that will annihilate whole populations overnight.
That the world might be simple and countable again.
  A village.
Or a handful of villages at peace with or killing each other.

III

There's the post-coital comfort of lying in bed after the storm.
The consolation my habitual self-image is unknown in
   the mirror.
That solemn eidolon I've fabricated from incense and
   candle oil.
I should mention I'm lying beside one awaiting the rapture.
Who's intoning the prayer. For only a small number are
   chosen.
Unless none are chosen. And tonight she is watching for
   a sign.
Something amid the turmoil of clouds, the ripped moonlight.
Just a small tear in the heavens as the storm clears will suffice.

A Carcass

from Baudelaire

Let's not forget the thing we saw, my soul,
    that morning when on the path ahead
we found carrion already turning foul
    under the sun on a gravel bed.

With legs raised, like a bold woman aroused,
    smouldering and emitting gas,
there in broad daylight shamelessly exposed
    lay the nude, bloated carcass.

On this spectacle the sun continued to blaze,
    grilling patiently till done
a dish Nature would devour and erase
    all she amassed and fused as one.

And the sky regarded that proud carcass
    as though it opened into flower –
the stench so strong you fainted to the grass,
    such was its odious power.

Bluebottles were buzzing round the abdomen,
    from which in tiny spits and spatters
maggots spewed and formed a molten column
    across the skin that hung in tatters.

The thing was neither resting nor at peace
    but wave-like seemed to swell and slide
as if the flesh, stirred by the morning breeze,
    was still alive and multiplied.

This busy mound was making eerie music
    like water rushing or the wind,
or grain at harvest yielding its soft acoustic
    when sifted through the reaper's hand.

Those forms – in a dream – were now growing fainter,
    an under-sketch hard to detect
abandoned on the canvas, which the painter
    from memory must perfect.

Nearby among some rocks a snarling bitch
    looked on with rabid eyes, and stood
stubborn while waiting for the chance to snatch
    a scrap she's left behind half-chewed.

Imagine love! You'll come to the same dung,
    this same disgusting confection,
my bright star, and sovereign of my tongue,
    my angel and my grand passion.

Aye! That'll be you one day, dear queen of grace,
    when you've received viaticum,
when you've been rubbed with herbs and sweet spice
    to clothe your body's new perfume.

Then, my beauty! tell the grubs who commence
    inscribing you with loving kisses
how I preserve the form and divine essence
    of love as my love decomposes.

The Narcissist

I've never been the type for looking in mirrors.
I'll check a mole. I shave. I wore contacts in my twenties.
I had a girlfriend back there who liked us to pose full-length.
Better than porn she said. But I couldn't look or not for long.
It's because of your *emptiness within* she whispered.

I was the narcissist. And it's true, all my life I've harboured
this selfie in my head . . . one that's blurry and soft-focus.
It must have been implanted early on by my mother.
I mean something cherubic but essentially featureless.
And though it's aged it has kept its original nullity.

Do you psychoanalysts have an angle on this?
Is it mellifluously dissected in Gallic abstraction?
Whenever I'm caught off-guard, in a hotel or new bedroom,
it comes as a shock I'm in the presence of another male,
who is florid and badly proportioned. But not repulsive.

This morning in a dream that came when I dozed off
between tweets, I found myself high above the *Diagonal*.
Back with that ex in an *ático* – my old old girlfriend
who trained me to love food and sip cognac, to appease
lapdogs and night porters, wear shades, relax in a fast car.

She'd brought along her props in a little crocodile case.
The music was on. Bowie I think – though the sound was
     distorted.
I could hear her intakes of breath and smell her warm skin.
Then I opened my eyes as instructed. Or dreamed I did.
I understood what I saw in the mirror was my corpse.

The Seven Songs of Myself

No dainty dolce affettuoso I

1

Every morning I get myself out of bed.
Every morning I scrub, I shave, I shine my teeth.
I check mail, Twitter, inner and outer weather.
I sip tea, look in the garden, throw pellets to the fish.
I swallow seven pills. I do my stretches. I run.
And think of friends, the living and the dead.
Every morning I phone one or other of my kids.

2

Every week I regret some portion of my life.
Every week I dream about my sainted mother.
I check over my skin. Step on the scales. Clean out the bins.
In spring I tape birdsong and trap snails in plastic
    containers.
In autumn I photograph spider webs on the rhododendron.
In winter I observe the constellations of the heavens.
I google remedies, Antarctic cruises, Tibetan hikes.
I contemplate a course in Mandarin or medieval French.
I google porn sites and download more Bugs Bunny.
I go over my boyhood deeds or nurse my grievances.
Every week I either call my sister or forget to.

3

Every so often I revise my position on the soul.
Every so often I imagine a maggot in the porridge of
     my brain.
Or I see my soul struggle like the fly in marmalade.
I see it change to a wind-borne creature in the sullen
     morning light.
I see the aggregate of life is a turbulent landless ocean.
And therein I am no more (no worse) than an agitated ion.
I see the coiling ocean is itself the beast biting its tail.
The divide between our selves and – as Eriugena saw and
     maybe Hart Crane – the Divine.
I read back over old copybooks and diaries.
I write down the names of pets, sailboats, schoolmates.
I remember the lake. Or I remember the farm.
I veer between Vedic calm and occidental strife.
I re-read the *Inferno* or I listen to the Book of Job.
Every so often I declare a change of mind or heart.

4

Elsewhere the mutagen is at large in the biochemical ocean.
Elsewhere the mutilated text and the doctored sample.
The toxic cell slipping through the pacified conurbation.
The ghost life of gland, synapse. The lung's persistent Morse.
The reflex thump, the mental snap, the horn-blare of fever.
The sorrows in the culvert that runs beneath the bypass.
As eyes dilate. As ears stay open. Skin assumes the heat
     or cold.
Elsewhere the seizure sulks – or is strapping on a vest.
Elsewhere the sibylline codes are writ on acid.
Altogether elsewhere the grainy herds of reindeer. The old
     migrations.

5

Some days I wake chemically selflessly content.
Some days I wake god bless me with a bone.
I wake with a song in my heart and a skip in my step.
I wake and to the shower I stride with a tune in my head.
Óró mo bháidín . . . I'm just a wild mountain rose!
There I am belting it out like I'm Dolly or Sinéad.
As the swan in the evening moves over the lake . . .
There I am with the soapy tears down my face.
There I am longing for the streets of Laredo.
For the two turtledoves or the six pretty maidens.
Once more *con affetto* now my lonesome days are over!
The wings of the dawn light. The sight of my true love.
And this morning I am whistling *Possente spirto.*
I'm begging the handsome boatman to ferry me over.
Óró this morning *Orfeo son io . . .* I am Orpheus.
Who failed not for his music but for a moment of doubt.

6

(laudation)

Of all sights, a new moon. Of all smells, bread. Of all
surfaces, skin.
Of all sweet sounds, the mourning dove and the sleeping
child.
Of all my journeys, the shortcut from school through
Buckley's Glen.
Of all other journeys, the Greyhound bus at night into
Manhattan.
Of cities, Jerusalem. Of modes of transport, the pony and car.
Of the neglected virtues, shyness. Of the celebrated,
hospitality.
Of harmless vices . . . the lie-in, the painted toe, the keepsake.
Of solitary vices, the night out and a piss in moonlight.

Of the social pastimes, gossip among cultivated friends.
Of the cultivars, either the grape or the apple.
Of the apples, the Wyken Pippin. Of cults, the Eleusinian.
Of all that delights the cultivated mind, letter-writing.
Of all jokes, the one about the two thieves.
Of practical jokes, the shoulder tap (oldest and most cruel).
Of all of Job's afflictions, maybe the boils.
Of terms of abuse *hypocrite*. Of terms of praise *musical*.
Of beverages, tea. Of all that coarsens the palate, eating beef.
Of ingenious devices, the search engine and the zip.
Of all that thrives among Satan's noisome progeny, the rock
    drill and mosquito.
Of the proofs of God's love, the crow.
Of all that testifies to the sway of evil, the white lie.
Of the forgotten sins, calumny (which thrives).
Of the erotic side-pleasures, the smile. And the text.
Of rare and elusive flavours, sweet cicely and the
    chanterelle.
Of domesticated creatures, the pig or goose.
Of all times, the hour before sunrise. Of all fears, the lump.
Of all places, here and now. Of sweet sounds to wake to,
    the mourning dove.

7

Blessings of Whitsun on the bash at full blast at the
    British Legion.
Blessings of the rain on the dog turds on the cobbles.
On the thrushes stabbing the snails on the mud-verges.
On the hoodies on the mopeds moping on the pavements.
On the trafficker and on the dealer and on the punter.
On the merchant screwing the farmer screwing the
    migrants.
Blessings on the online ego-merchants on Facebook etc.
On the troll trolling the lone wolf or the pack-hunters.

On the mob with Argus eyes – the detractors of character.
On those proclaiming the way and the supremacy of
    the Way.
On the hordes descending on the ports and on the airports.
On the multitudes gathered on the mountains and on
    the plains.
On the dust of the plain and the wind of the impassable
    mountain.
Blest be those who curse the hour we were borne to such
    a pass.
Curst be the righteous. Curst be the whitèd sepulchres.
    Curst be the Just.
Blessings on my neighbour. On her streetwise kids. On the
    street cleaner.
Blessings of Whitsun on the wedding or wake still on at
    the Legion.

Hamartia

We each have our tragedy. Yours, she's telling me to my face,
is my fixation on the local. I nod.
(We are, after all, in the Pyrotechnists Arms).
You know what I mean! Those litanies of place names.
And besides you're stuck in some wormhole.
Band names. Brand names. Dead girlfriends.
You can only drink out of a straight pint glass.
You can only sleep on clean white sheets.
You boil pigs' feet and eat Golden Wonders in their skins.
Nothing's to your liking unless you had it moons ago.

It's true I like to sleep on freshly laundered linen.
Though one time, believe me, things were pretty hairy.
I slept between menhirs high above the Atlantic.
On a Chesterfield in the penthouse of a Park Plaza.
I was on the lookout for my life's calling. A crusade.
I'd Africa in mind. Child poverty. River blindness.
The last surviving pair of northern white rhino.
I'd one foot on the gangplank of a boat bound for Mombasa.

O Brave New World that had such novels in it!
You sold out. You turned sour. You went to seed.
You've become this old gasser full of wind and sentiment.
Her index finger is prodding my ribcage.
Gently now, as though I'm an endangered species.
You're a throwback, a quisling, a swipe left, a a a
I'm nodding again. At everything she has to tell me.

The Surly Boy

I've parked the hire car next the pumps and wait.
Wait for the bell to chime and out come the surly fair-haired
    boy.
To whom I'll shout *fill her to the brim with juice.*

Over the road a curtain twitches in the early breeze.
Trish must've spotted me and's thinking *I've time to change
    my top.*
But hey, here she is at the car window leaning in.

Nice jeep! she's saying and *there's a hop tonight in Charleville.*
A cloud of musk afloat in the valeted air.
But the boy's gone to his supper. That shop looks shut for
    the night.

And now the padlock's on and hey, the Mobil's lost its ruby 'o'.
Somewhere I must've known the surly boy took wing to
    farm sheep
in New South Wales – and Trish moved to the Glebe.

Under the hardstanding the tank's a cave of fumes.
I've half a mind to jemmy the manhole cover.
And get *ah* that oletime whiff of sulphur up my nose.

The Prefect Boy

Now I'd a cell to call my own – a chair and desk,
a rad whereto I flung my hurling gear
after the three-hour scrum in rain and mire –
I bought a bunch of Penguin Modern Classics
and ranged them on the ledge, as I warm to the task
of becoming, in this my sixteenth year,
Rimbaud redivivus – a whitèd sepulchre
whose deliquescent brain's a Kafkaesque
conundrum to the Dean when he raids the dorm
to find one *oh so fallen into pallid ennui*
with book in hand – and not consoling, say, the auburn
French maid still on her knees, in tears, in the ball alley.
Sacerdotal, I'm holding aloft my *Franny and Zooey*.
A nod, he's gone. Then back to check it isn't porn.

Topology

Limerick Junction

No, we hadn't seen the film but without a doubt
that's me in the teashop waiting. Waiting it seems
for my teacup to turn to a doughnut. And here you are
turning up, wobbly I can see, and for an hour
we're watching through plate glass the almost-silent
comedy of a pair of forklifts grunting and shunting
at flatcars, all the novelty of boxed cargo
(the word containerisation is unknown to us).
Then you rip open my package and gasp at the image –
scared and beautiful, far too hard ever to erase.
Then yes, you stand on those clogs, since the stars
or the maths have snipped our parts from the plot.
But leaving all the same this shadow on my lifeline.
Since there it was for a heartbeat, the doughnut,
before resuming the semblance of handle and cup.

Monopoly

Ed Smart has just uttered the word *décolletage*,
reminding us all of last night's episode
with Nyree Dawn Porter as Emma Bovary.
Ed's eyes are glued to the strapless cream top wherein
Trish's new breasts are devising
so many rules I've become confused
whether to mortgage Kings Cross or pass.

'Ngaire', the Little White Flower of the Maori,
was named for Thérèse of Lisieux –
the girl who never would
remove her clothes, not even for Kenneth More as
    Cousin Jolyon,
would never know she brought sin into Lisgoold
that summer when Ed and I were rolling the dice
to stop perilously close to the peach-cream top wherein etc.

Trish, who the other day stopped me dead on Bond Street
with a wavering gold-encircled hand.
She had run off with a stockbroker, or a pawnbroker,
and they'd rented down in Putney
(where Nyree, too, would see out her sunset years).
The shop was sold, the old place gone to ruin.
An almost famous writer now lived in the Glebe.

I was holed up myself out in the Chilterns.
Aiai! I had a train to catch from Marylebone.
Again we parted company.
Ed is *smart*, she taunted me, and it's true
he soon won the game, though I still like to think
for him she never lifted the top wherein etc.
as she did that once for me.

Madame Bovary

I'm following the old man out to Clonmult.
That's him bareback on the mare, his head
in a cloud of hawthorn, taking her to stud.
I'm in the Morris behind, stalling
and starting, with *Madame Bovary*
propped open on the dashboard.

Nance, the mare, is my small sister, hand-
reared with the Pyrex bottle
and rubber teat I'd barely surrendered.
In the paddock, the black stallion is up
on his hindquarters, wielding his yard
like it's a length of plastic hosepipe.

Now it's done, we switch roles –
that's me on Nance belting for home,
while my father is gone to the East
on his travels, off on a batter,
Madame Bovary at Chapter Twelve,
yellowing under the windshield.

#PoorMe

Born into the Dark Age of the two-stroke generator
with an orphaned foal for sibling, who shared my milk
and mother's affection – who in my infancy witnessed
the crucifixion of pigs, the beheading of a goose,
the execution of the show-horses under the linden,

barefoot I walked to chapel and school, was reared
without running water, music or the favour of grace,
brought up among corner boys, vets and sadists,
educated by a gang of potato-patch fornicators,
at fifteen guilt became my middle name – whereupon
I found a naked woman in a foreign magazine.

I have endured night-sweats, migraines, fear of clouds
and airborne insects, the hourly stabs of self-loathing.
And have come to suffer the seven types of ambivalence
including whether to be buried in oak or in cardboard,
to rot in loam or limestone or better just ascend in smoke.

And whether to make an online deathbed confession?
A last-gasp cleansing of the soul – one last cliffhanger.
But no, I will go to my makers unshaven and unshriven,
face my mother and the long line of my mothers in
    headscarves
and floral aprons, nodding and passing judgement.
Who want nothing to do with the fruit of their womb.

The Damned Soul

from Old English

'Listen, skinbag, small heed you paid,
in your pursuit of ease and pleasure,
to the eternity in store for your soul
after I was banished from the body.
It would be better, mudball, for us both
had you been born a mute fish or a bird,
or if only you'd lived the life of an ox
and foraged for food on the ground,
grazed with goats carefree in the fields.
Or had you been one of the wild beasts,
a bear or wolf bred in the wilderness,
even a despised poisonous snake,
that would have proved a preferable fate
to being created human. And been baptised.'

Thus the soul complains. The body stays dumb.
It can no longer draw in air or devise words.
The head is loose, the limbs are helpless.
The mouth gapes and the gums fester.
Muscle and fat turn mouldy and rancid.
Worms are wriggling inside the rib cage,
their jaws avid, eager with appetite,
as they hurry to satisfy long hunger.
They don't pause for talk and pleasantries.
Guzzler is the name of their General,
the wriggler in charge with the razor teeth.
He attacks the tongue, bores into the jawbone,
eats the soft lids shielding the eyes,
opens a path to the organs, the prime meat,
burrows a way through to the gut's banquet.

Barely has the body, long used to luxury,
gone cold than it becomes itself a tasty dish.
Food for worms. Let this serve as fair warning,
a reminder to men, who want wisdom.

Shoulder Tap

Matty, in memory

I'm walking along the towpath though also
peering into the undergrowth it seems beside
the Leamlara (in Irish *Léim Lárach*, the Mare's Leap)
– a slur on, I'm thinking, the little river where
with the tip of a finger he's keeping my body afloat
until he laughs and seeing he's yards upstream
I go under kicking like a calf – that's to say
I'm years away when I hear the voice, soft and cajoling,
dwell on my name – then the tap on my shoulder.
And I swing in sudden anger to fuck at him.
The oldest trick in the book . . . and I've fallen for it.

The Prodigal

for Matthew Sweeney

The chime of a clock from a darkened room
downstairs, some hushed recess . . . it speaks
of polished wood, lightly oiled gears,
the brush of slippered feet that come
at dusk, a hand's swift chamois wipe.
The port decanter rests on the TV –
a house where the old die with their beads,
the light trembling by the Virgin's shrine.

Once were angry words: a door slammed
and a car revved in the startled grounds,
then roared away. I tap the oak barometer
in the hall, and pat the blind foxhound
who raises his nose to sniff my trousers
before going back to his hunting dream.

Feet

in memory

We were sitting in the restaurant window
when I heard myself say *Seamus is here* –
though there was no greeting. And our view was blocked
by the brewery lorry mounted on the kerb.
I'd no sight of him. But it was nothing spooky either.
What I had seen under the lorry were two feet
passing on the other side. I'd known him by the gait,
as one would by the voice. Yet I'd never before
noticed his feet – and, if asked, I might have guessed
he had a fisherman's walk, slow and deliberate.
But no, what I saw were the feet of a schoolboy
invisibly sandaled, stepping nimbly towards us.

Yeomen

Moses or Pharaoh has been with me all year,
January to January, haunting the landing.
At night when I pad down the stairs for a drink,
one of them steps to the side. No sound or touch,
just a slight drop in temperature as I go past.
At the fridge, I hear bullocks wheezing on the slabs.
As I step out to piss, an owl screeches in flight
and I spot the Dioscuri in the branches of the elm.
Brothers christened for a laugh, or in ignorance?
One twin – Pharaoh or Moses – died on the Marne
and is remembered on a stone in the churchyard.
The other stands guard outside my bedroom at night.

The Moment

I'm carrying it upstairs like a very hot cup of coffee.
I'm thinking ahead to the bedroom while at the back of my
    mind
there's another room, vaguely a receding series of rooms –
which means I'm missing the 3D torrent of the moment
(but at least the coffee hasn't spilled).

If it were raining out, I'd try to think of every drop
on every roof tile in Willesden, then on all the farmland to
    the west
and out over the Irish Sea, where I'd observe
the volcanic bubbling and speeded-up eruption
of an angry rash on the troughs between waves

until the brain's graphene stretched to the graveyard
where yesterday we stood around in the wet.
But now this morning the sun is out.
I try to think of a star spending into space its photonic roar,
only a decimal point of which is stopped by the earth

and nil, statistically speaking, fills the day outside,
where the leaves of the plane trees are a zillion keyboards
clicking it into chlorophyll.
Better hold off the moment. Let the coffee go cold.
Then can the brain dip into what's occurred.

The Jailbird

I've this gut feeling that inside somewhere,
perched, so to speak, in the innermost wood
of my body or brain, on mute since childhood
a bird-creature lurks in its cramped lair
for when the wood's consumed, as in a fire,
though also consumed as drinks are or food
(over months or could be years ingesting crude
chemicals, making the sly one ever slyer).
But then crackle 'n' pop, it's all gone for good.
And good riddance, since freed from its bonds
the avian now preens its wings and absconds
from the scene below (that's me, in my last throes)
skyward like a lark saying fuck to the whole brood
and piping forth a blithe hymn as she goes.

Lumps

Spoiling the gravy, lumps.
In my cup *please, just the one.*
Still in bed at noon, the lump.
Check one side, then the other.
Often in the throat, a lump.

The Third Wish

My last was the Soul's last draught – the taste almost
    remembered – of the Body's elixir.
And so it is – it's blind chance – I'm outside the canted
    walk-up block on Main St West braced
and maybe kept in place by, on the roof, a giant
    billboard telling me this blue morning
I've *come to where the flavor is*. Marlboro Country.
    Not a soul in sight. Signs everywhere.
A Sprite gone flat on the table, on the turntable Blondie's
    Call Me. Bathwater scuzzy. Cold.
And now in the airshaft *Arum dem fayer* – next door's
    pure contralto while she showers.
I break open a Molson X, slide on *Nighthawks*,
    twirl the channels . . . hockey, the seal hunt,
Carter's twitching face, an angry blackclad chorus – kid
    on a metal leg running in a blizzard
                            Shoyn genug
In bafflement and loneliness I betake my lithe,
    my featherlite Mark Spitz new bod,
East to Hanrahan's and fall in with Bob Kennedy
    theonetheydidntshoot on Shuffleboard.
We take on the bleary night shift in from Stelco.
    Truckers off the 403. Skinning them,
Bob pocketing our bets to buy Su and Gipsy
    – over for the week from Buffalo –
shots between their sets. *And donate the Cancer Kid.*
    Dude with steel peg on that fool run.
Cross the whole goddammit country! I hop it to the can,
    donate my last quarter to the payphone
only to hear it ring out once more.

Thunder

as I unfurl into *what a night.* Jog
along Barton in a downpour, the Expressway
    a glazed arcade I ghost across to locate
the mudtrack through Cootes Paradise, and home past
    the dismantled elms, the Bowling Green,
where a moonstruck she-chuck's brought her kits
    where a month ago or one before
we made angels. I stop for a puff beside the Shul
    but ma chuck's wise to my perfume.
I give the Jesus sign and slip away. Sneak a leak
    back of Mike's Submarines, then hit
the hay as swollen-fingered dawn ignites a bonfire
    inside the Lake. And fall in a swound.

Hello (a seamless join) she's softly in
the doorframe, all smiles. All planned it seems. *Weekend
    out West* with Bunny and with Mum.
A clutch under her oxter of dog-eared term papers.
    But the noon sky above Marlboro Country's
skyblue and we scarper diem up the escarpment,
    bumping bikes along beside the railroad,
she in cut-off jeans and cotton top – where a sweat map
    unfolds as we lean into the climb.
And a Canadian Pacific's pulling past us uphill slow
    heading for the heartlands – we hoick
the bikes onto an empty flatcar. Lifts us over the brow.

Should we have stayed aboard? Bound
for the Sault and Thunder Bay, found a door to other lives
    or vanished in the boreal sublime . . . ?
Thing is you haven't a clue. You're in the thick of moods.
    Swings. The grip of some MacGuffin.
And every ego-punch and knockdown, each rare sweet trade,

all the aggregate of being true or kind,
is not a blank (since nothing in the end surprises us).
    The face on the pillow. Our kids' twin-flame.
Those suited folk on the concourse who wave and smile.
    One who seems to look into the soul.
Even the half-heard newsflash fits some jigsaw dream.
    But we're untuned. There's noise. No frame.
What to make of these muscle-bound cars along the street?
    While the Scotty or Jean-Luc zipping by
isn't jet propelled but on a Schwinn! While the same mustard
    school bus stands next the Mission Church.

We lower the bikes onto fireweed and break into woods
    above Dundas. Pick out the Indian trail.
Bluejays scuffle in the brush. Blades of light dazzle
    the treetops . . . a rose-breast grosbeak in flight?
While woodpeckers camouflaged in chequered shade

                              hammer out
    a half-remembered code . . . but it fades.
The grove is hushed and we push on through pine litter
    in rustling silence, then watch ourselves
emerge. Revenants behind the new developments.
    From where it's downhill back to Mike's.
Me now on good old mudguardless brakeless 'baldie'
    (I got it for a song one Harvest Fayre),
my sneakers sparking off asphalt as we round each bend.
    There's burn each side of the back strap
and beads of – mercury, honeydew? – across her spine.
    Or rivulets of rain . . . run-stop sideways
retrieved from an InterCity window outside Leeds.

It's *Smokey*'s last day at the Westdale,
a line along the sidewalk to Piccone's ice-cream.
    Dust-devils shimmy in the car lot.
We sprint for the screen door, take the stairs' rungs three
    at a time, a footrace to the icebox,
a dead heat to our little room – the bed let's not forget
    pledged to Chris the basement medic,
Christophe and Marta, or Maria, his Coptic bride,
    tapping her bump the very day the Kid
pulls out of his run (losing a fight he's also won)
    and storms break from Huron to the Gulf.
Chris-smiling-signing-Marta make angels on our bed.
    They like its royal fit. We nudge them
to its purchase, then give it them for free. For love.
    The island place we rowed to in our dream.
Whence through an eyelet of the night I'm whisked away.

With (a) Little Help from Rainer Maria Rilke

I woke a changed man. My balls alive, my brain alive. Full
    of dread.
Him drawing the spunk up into an abrupt rapturous tree.
Spasms of intensity that are soon thinned by memory.
But the dreams with the compound eye comprehend them.
Someone I'd loved who was East European strode in in
    gold trousers.
Sweet Jesus how the old cock crowed! Though I was *niet*
    for her.
I guess drop dead gorgeous 25 she likes me a lot but.

Those were the years of privation and shamefulness.
Nosing around? Some. My poor soul unfit for purpose.
But in the depths of the Abyss quite a cheerful bit of river.
If only I could live by that . . . *had* lived by it, I'd be a better
    person.
The nicest thing of all is the spurting of water.
When inside my clothes the figure of the god stands gentle
at the crossroads. My stiff corpse again growing soft.

Bugs Bunny to the Rescue

Some folks have called me cocky and brash.
They're saying I'm way too big for my boots.
In actual fact, I'm just *totally* self-possessed.
I'm nonchalant, unflappable, a contemplative.
I play it cool, man – though I do get hot under the collar.
I know all the ups and downs, twists and turns of the game.
And the game is all about the beauty of the chase.
I chomp on my carrot the same reason Groucho chomps on
  his cigar.
It stops me rushing too fast into the next routine.
See, I've long figured I'm appearing in an animation.
When it looks like I'm cornered and done for – don't you be
  consoined.
I've always got one more dodge up my . . . um sleeve.
It weally is only a big put-on when I scweam!
Let's face it, Doc, I've read the script. I know how it turns out.

Slatterns

a cento for Angela Dufresne

When I first met Angela she was painting landscapes

Copulating couples were hidden in *Where's Waldo?* style

Freud, or a generic white-bearded psychiatrist, occasionally makes an appearance

At times the artist features herself

The Villa Huppert for the Passage of Macedonia (2005) is an imagined holiday home for Isabelle Huppert

There's a small painting inspired by *Rear Window* (a film so much about the gaze) and a number of drawings from that era of Angela's career

Woman on woman, man on man, woman on man, celebrities and film stars anachronistically paired in strange architectural monstrosities

The figures stirred in me an inexplicable sense of identification

& I found, to my surprise, I was weeping

Sainthood

This fledgling – a house or tree sparrow – shows no fear of me.
Perches on the trellis, then onto the rain barrel. Far too close.
Giving shrill cheeps, and tilting its bud head with an enquiry
at each cheep. Does it want to be fed? Or just being chummy?
Neither, for sure. Poor creature's lost, barely fledged, a
    hormone
hasn't yet kicked in. *This is it. Flight. Distances. Blue open sky.*
I keep dead still, fancying myself a bit of a Saint Francis.
And indeed the bird soon flies over and hovers against the wall
of my chest, picking at it, thinking maybe there it will find
    a nest.

Terrace

The same signature tune next door, and down the street
    the same argument – ye olde refrain since Adam.
While kids grow up along the terrace in rooms where shades
    of paint and wallpaper fade and reappear
according to a sequence they share with molluscs – or else
    the river's length over distance travelled.

So our million lives are the same life all bound into one
    exploding rose, and the lamp burns decades hence
at just this tilt, the Brazilian twins scoot past the window
    and a spear of humid African air ignites
the sunset behind the train rigs, while the tune continues
    never-ending binding us with tongues of fire.

New from Next Door

Lying here I hear *Hallelujah! Hallelujah!*
Loud through the party wall – neither sung nor chanted
but hammered out. Either a desperate lullaby
or desperate exorcism. Either one will do.

The Billboard

Ladders shooting up, boots on the roof, our little room
    shaking.
Shouts in the airshaft of – what we take to be – Ukrainian.
What doom has overtaken us in sleep? Then we figure it.
A work crew has come to change the ad on the billboard.
On the huge billboard that braces and holds the roof in place.

We're stuck. Nothing for it but make love while it goes on.
And by the time we finish things are normal again. Just about.
They're loading the van and driving off with strips of the
    old board.
Which we recall displayed ski gear. Now we're under a new
    sign.
And soon it will be time to cross the street and learn what it is.

Mould

Nature in the biological realm has a tendency to be fanciful
— FREEMAN DYSON

The mould on this six-week-old tomato sauce
has grown a green merino fleece with glints
of blue and orpiment and – now I blow over it –
a sheen of luminescence like an uncut hayfield.

I hesitate before ditching it, as I would a goldfish.
Or the drooping cactus. This isn't just food gone bad
but an organism with (I think) genes and enzymes.
Far more than the chemistry of rot or ferment.

It quadrupled while we were off over-exposing
our pink skins. Jumping from the dock, whooping it up
round the barbecue, loving each other, then rowing
over loos and ice trays. Before hugging again.

Just about keeping the lid on the id, as our guts
settled into microbial harmony and we grew back
into the old us swearing and farting in chorus.
Gruntled swine. Among God's simpler creatures.

While here in the fridge dark something mycelial,
artful, got under way – its own notion of culture
determined, while sensitive to initial conditions.
And now how gratuitous, and pretty, the outcome.

There we lay splayed on the deck, our skins maybe
experimenting with UV but young forever we were.
Here the pure carry-on. No plan or purpose. Or the plan
obscured in riddles of symmetry and equilibrium.

I blow again across the summer meadow. I take a pic.
One to post! Clickable. Squiggly, like a late Pollock.
And sort of tasty-looking, though it would kick up
a spectacular shit-storm in the jetlagged family gut.

So *nice try mate* down you go! In a swirl of rainbows
into carbolic suds and boiling water – a foul dybbuk
sputtering in the plughole for a fiery moment . . .
Then that rattle as you're sluiced beyond the U-bend.

Gravel

for Frank

I, too, will spend an hour playing with the gravel.
Sorting and cleaning it. It does love the dirt.
Dead leaves, grit, seeds that can sprout. And it hides
the odd slug or worm. We can't be having that!
Some of these stones have come a great distance.

I can no longer tell which are from Uist or Orkney.
And there's one came from a mountain in Sarawak.
Could it be this basalt with the twinkle of schist?
A shame. It's somehow joined the rabble tipped
here one morning from the Travis Perkins lorry.

I'm acting the snob! Each and every anonymous stone
has its captive soul, its own fixed little being.
And stones are time travellers. They start out in lake
  or esker,
or on the seafloor having housed small creatures.
The very tips of the Himalayas are limestone.

All these mute souls, who can tell their journeys . . .
How can I be their god! I'm too bald to be a saviour.
Though for an hour we'll sift them through our hands.
Each one – like the last poems of Celan – born dark.
Each one condemned for the duration of the earth.

Song before My Birth

after Laforgue

Jacked, I am! Plough on,
keep hacking at these tangled sticky roots
even though, Mother-dear, it's your innards!
Must make it to the light, to the awful promise
   of a sunrise!

Everybody gets just the one shot. And soon I'll sail
radiant out of limbo, an immaculate soul!

   Plough on!
A close call I had, but now I'm slaloming along,
the sun on my tail! Dribbling with nectar and cream.
Off to bye-byes I'll go on these voluptuous clouds,
   one of the gods!

Dream what you like out there! I'm the dark one
who'll hide in windblown skirts like I'm alone.

   Plough on!
No more sleepy-byes on the milk-roads of heaven.
No more naps beneath God's blue and starry eyes.
I'm falling head-over-heels into a land of virile juice.
    Easy does it now.
   Righto! I'm almost through . . .

I'll take the Sacrament, my head swivelled to the East.
Sure I will, in the guise of new illicit intimacies.

Plough on!
Let the bells toll! Let the solar flares filter in!
Adieu, sunken forests! In whose sheltering weed
my bud took hold, my timorous soul found heat.
Do I already feel death's chill? Plough on!
Ahoy, Mother!

Nurse, latch me now and forever to the breast.
It's time this infant prodigy began to feast.

The Beach Poem

He shall deliver thee from the snare of the fowler
– Psalms 91:3

Empty. Not quite. A couple and what could be an Irish
    wolfhound
are dots behind. Ahead nothing but sand curving into itself,
its vanishing point hidden in a daub of cloud and sea-mist.
'Strand' I'd say back home, land's end and abandonment,
    though not
on this daft tectonic scale. The wind in my face must be
    force five.
But leaning into it I enjoy the exertion. The feeling it gives
I'm being punished, and withstanding it, stokes up a fire
    inside.

There's nothing Attenborough-ish, nothing televisual about
the ocean's scrolling surfaces. And the beach to me is a dull
shelving track strewn with shells, sea wrack and bones of
    birds.
Sand dollars – what a delightful thought! Where would
    I look?
Sea urchin. Lugworm. Ghost shrimp. Words for creatures
    I don't know.
And then those scales beyond (the fleas on bigger fleas)
    with such things
as copepods, the soups of protozoa . . . to all of that I'm blind.

Like Van Gogh who loved spirals and saw them in skies
 and cornfields
but not in sunflowers – where my grandson points to them
 (and yells!).
He (Vincent) paints gaudy decorations in which, up close,
 the seed heads
are an ochre mud I've had the child-like urge to put my
 finger in.
Out here he'd have found the whirling spaces of his
 naked brain
projected in the labyrinths of living things, in vortices of
 sky and water.
And the cycles of sand and rock on those grand
 unhuman scales.

All of which thank god to me is veiled. A few seabirds
 are scissoring
the canvas, diving oh so routinely – no panic lads! Idlers
 like ourselves,
sure the shelves are packed with food and will pester us
 with choice.
I've driven here to find a green crab shell (to bring home
 for a friend).
He loves a poem it's in and for miles it appears this shelf
 doesn't have one.
Then there's loads, though only fragments, like shattered
 porcelain.
But I find a perfect specimen of an even more exquisite
 speckled kind.

And now holding it imagine, like the poet, the creature
    that lived in it,
whose existence must have been a constant ever-panicked
    whirr or hum
(like my schoolboy Sony after closedown resonating with
    empty space).
It could have felt something near to how I feel these nights
    when drifting
in and out of dreams, listening in warmth to the almost-
    silence of the land.
Snug and complete it was. But it's not here, utterly not!
    Gone without
a trace. Except it's in that poem with its wishful thinking.
    Sort of.

Oh to be gone *just like that* (Tommy Cooper). Or walk on
    and get whittled down
by wind or dissolve in the percussive salty light, not to go
    back over the same
sameness over back to the car (which the kid at the rental
    pestered me to choose).
But when I turn, surprise! A bird takes a fancy to me. Yes,
    this *is* courtship!
Its coming close, then flitting off. Teaser. I proffer a few
    sweet nothings.
Soothe our lonely hearts, little bird – stay and be my pal!
    But off she flies.
Done with the game. Adieu deceiving elf . . . I'm done, too.
    Puffed.

It's a blessing to reach the car (a chirpy Scandi hybrid) and
    it whips me back
before night falls to the Whaler's Inn, rigged out with shrouds
    and halyards,
where perched on Ahab's stool, I get tipsy on some Oregon
    fizz the bartender
tells me is 'ambrosial'. It's not but it makes me convivial. With,
    on my left, a man
who has a Slovene wife – snatched off the internet? He voted
    for the Turnip.
And, on my right, some old salt, a bore but heck at least a
    Democrat. We chew
the fat, we argue the toss. Concur on. Cyclists. Snowflakes.
    Time-travel.

Heck, I'm all reciprocity, not bored at all. The conversation
    does me good.

I Was Woken by the Leader of the Free World

flying over Willesden on his way to Hertfordshire.
For once I was having a nice dream. A gig or party.
With loads of youngsters in Docs and distressed jeans.
I was telling them a joke with a hilarious pun on turnip.
It doesn't translate but it had the room in stitches.

If you'd been looking in the upstairs window
– I seldom draw the curtains these clear winter nights –
you'd have caught the angelic smile on my sleeping face.
And maybe found yourself smiling back like my father used
when he hovered above my cot for me to wake.

Now the helicopters are thundering right overhead,
and I'm wide awake and scowling,
my father's turned away in angry disappointment.
I get out to watch the leader of the free world
become a silent birdlike dot in a glorious dawn sky.

(4 December 2019)

Questions for the Oracle

for Nadine Brummer

Will it rain? Will the hibiscus be in flower?
Will the boats arrive from Naros safe and on time?
Will Phillip come? With his new bride, Alcmene?
Will everything go according to plan
and everyone get along? No sulks or quarrels,
no tasteless jokes about the Christians?
And Penny, my dear friend who cannot come
– will this be the very night she gives birth?
Will it be a girl or a boy? Will it be born
without mishap, I pray, or too much pain?

Will Bella come? And Quintus behave
and not jump in the fish pond? Will everyone
get along? Will my husband frown at the sweetmeats,
the sauces, the wine? Will the food taste good anyway?
Will I be at ease with the wives, and avoid
nervously finishing their sentences?
Will Quintus give me a drunken kiss,
like he did a year ago? And those who've died since
be here? Saul, and my mother? And Simonides Rufus,
who teased me when we were children,
crucified six weeks ago in Smyrna?

Will the rain keep off, at least till night falls
when people come indoors? And Quintus play
the old tunes from the islands? My husband then
be full of fellowship and army gossip,
and this become one of those nights
the islanders talk of, recalling a time blest
by Demeter and by your kind light, Lord Apollo?

Notes

'The Prodigal' was written at the request of Matthew Sweeney some years before his death in 2018.

'The Third Wish' refers to Terry Fox, a 21-year-old cancer patient and amputee, who in 1980 attempted to run across Canada to raise money for cancer research. He set out on 12 April from St John's, Newfoundland, running the equivalent of a marathon per day. The spread of cancer forced him to abandon his run on 1 September outside Thunder Bay, Ontario, having completed two-thirds of the journey. He died a Canadian national hero on 28 June 1981.

'With (a) Little Help from Rainer Maria Rilke' combines images from dreams with lines and phrases from Rilke's 'phallic' poems.

'Bugs Bunny to the Rescue' recycles – via Wikipedia – material from Bob Clampett's 'What's Up Doc?', in *Draw the Looney Tunes: The Warner Brothers Character Design Manual*.

'Slatterns' is co-authored with Kathryn Maris using text from her introduction to the catalogue for the Slatterns Exhibition at the APT Gallery (2018). It was written for the 'Modern Couples with *Mal* Journal' event at the Barbican (18 January 2019), curated by Maria Dimitrova.

'Song before My Birth' resulted from a commission by Suzannah V. Evans for a translation project, funded by the T. S. Eliot Foundation, at Durham University.